This Feeling has Fangs and a Heartbeat

This is an IndieMosh book

brought to you by MoshPit Publishing
an imprint of Mosher's Business Support Pty Ltd

PO Box 4363
Penrith Plaza NSW 2750

indiemosh.com.au

Copyright © Cassie Mutch 2023

The moral right of the author has been asserted in accordance with the Copyright Amendment (Moral Rights) Act 2000.

All rights reserved. Except as permitted under the Australian Copyright Act 1968 (for example, fair dealing for the purposes of study, research, criticism or review) no part of this publication may be reproduced, stored in a retrieval system, or transmitted in any form or by any means, electronic, mechanical, photocopying, recording or otherwise, without the written permission of the publisher.

 A catalogue record for this work is available from the National Library of Australia

https://www.nla.gov.au/collections

Title:	This Feeling has Fangs and a Heartbeat
Author:	Mutch, Cassie (1996–)
ISBNs:	9781923065253 (paperback)
Subjects:	BODY, MIND & SPIRIT / Inspiration & Personal Growth FAMILY & RELATIONSHIPS / Love & Romance POETRY / Women Authors; General

No individual in these poems is taken from real life. Any resemblance to any person or persons living or dead is accidental and unintentional. The author, their agents and publishers cannot be held responsible for any claim otherwise and take no responsibility for any such coincidence.

Illustrated by Hayley Lye at hayleyclaireart.com

Cover concept by Cassie Mutch and Hayley Lye

Cover design and images by Hayley Lye

Cover layout by Sarah Davies at lemondesignstudio.com.au/

This Feeling has Fangs and a Heartbeat

Cassie Mutch

Contents

A SNIPPET xiii

FIRE

   GIRL IS NOT A DIRTY WORD 1

   TO THE BOY WHO THOUGHT HE COULD TAKE WHAT WASN'T HIS 2

   TO THE BOY WHO TOOK WHAT WASN'T HIS ... 3

   TO THE NO VOTERS 5

   MONSTER 6

   ROAD ACCIDENT 7

   A GIRL IN A WAITING ROOM 8

   NIGHTMARES ON PUBLIC TRANSPORT 10

   WONDER WOMAN PART 1 11

   SLIMY 12

   THIS DOUBT ISN'T YOURS 13

   INFERNO 14

   WEAPONS AGAINST THE WORLD 15

   EMOTIONAL BLADE 16

   TWO-FACED 17

   TELL IT TO THE GIRL WHO LOST SOMETHING 18

   SQUASHED 19

   PREDATOR 21

   CAREFULLY CRAFTED CAGES 22

   IN DEFENCE OF FANGS 24

FRIENDSHIP HURTS TOO 26
HOME HAS A HOLE IN IT 27

WATER

FANGED FEELINGS 31
DAILY BATTLEFIELD 32
LONELINESS WARMED UP 33
WAR AT SEA PART 1 34
WAR AT SEA PART 2 36
SYMPTOMS OF ACCIDENTALLY FEELING THINGS 38
COSTUME PARTY 39
GIRL 40
ORCHESTRA 41
450 DEGREES FAHRENHEIT 42
MUSINGS ON BODY 43
A SORT OF APOLOGY POEM 44
I WOULD CHOOSE PAIN 45
BIRTHDAY BLUES 46
GHOST OR GIRL? 47
YOU CAN'T HEAL BROKEN BOYS WITH YOUR HANDS 48
SURGERY ROOM 49
TOUCH 50
INSECT WINGS 51
I AM SO FUCKING SCARED 52
IT'S NOT YOU 54

PARALLEL WORLD	55
LONELY'S FAVOURITE	56
I CRAVE YOU STILL	57
DRESSED FOR DEFEAT	58
EROSION	59
UPROOT	60
SO LOUD	61
WHEN YOU'RE AWKWARD AF	62
DAYDREAM	63
SELF-PORTRAIT	64
CRUSH	65
SPARSE SANITY	66
A PLACE AT THE TABLE	67
WHAT IF MY BUS DOESN'T COME?	69
DAD	70
ADVANCED APOLOGY	71
IN THIS WORLD I AM ALIVE	73
GRIEF IS AN EMPTY SPACE	74
FISSURES	75
THE FOOL	76
BOYS BUILT BY THE PATRIARCHY	77
I WISH I COULD STOP WRITING ABOUT YOU	78
YOU MAKE MY BRAIN MALFUNCTION	79
ALIEN	80
EGGSHELL SKIN	81

ME VS MY BRAIN...... 82

I KEEP SEEING YOU...... 83

EARTH

TODAY...... 87

SWEET AUTUMN 88

HOME 90

AFTERNOON ON TWO WHEELS...... 91

CRAVINGS...... 92

SEA OF SUNFLOWERS 93

PLANT POWER...... 94

THE FIRST SUNDAY IN OCTOBER...... 95

LOVE LETTER TO THE EARTH 96

CATHARSIS...... 97

SUMMER IGNORANCE 98

STILLNESS 99

SUMMER SKIN 100

DELAYED MAIL...... 101

MYTH...... 102

HOMEBODY ON THE MOON 103

SUMMER'S NIGHT 104

MAGIC SPELLS 105

AUTUMN 106

I THOUGHT I WAS BETTER...... 108

STARDUST 109

TUNNEL VISION...... 111

APPLE TREE 112

POEMS WRITTEN ON BUSES 114

15 OCTOBER 2018 115

THE SPACE BETWEEN BREATHS 116

AIR

WISHLIST 121

NOTE TO SELF 122

WISHLIST IN NOVEMBER 2017 123

I WILL NEVER KEEP YOU FROM YOURSELF 124

THINGS I LOVED THIS WEEK 125

GREY 126

WONDER WOMAN PART 2 127

WOLF 128

COOL GIRL 129

EPIPHANIES 130

LET THE PAST SLEEP 131

YOU WILL FEEL WARM AGAIN 132

FIZZING SODA 133

UNDRESS YOUR FEAR 134

CONFESSIONS 135

I AM ALONE 136

PASSENGER SEAT 137

IF I COULD SKETCH 138

TUNE IN 140

MOVING PIECES 141

GROWTH 142

3PM 143

THIS BODY IS YOURS	144
GROWING PAINS	145
A SKETCH FROM MY IMAGINATION	146
HAPPY PRIDE	148
IT'S LIKE THIS	149
ACKNOWLEDGEMENTS	150
ABOUT THE AUTHOR	151
ABOUT THE ARTIST	152

For anyone who has ever felt like maybe the wires in their brain are a little frayed around the edges.

A SNIPPET

Before you delve further into this book, I should give you a sense of what is ahead. I started writing poems when I was 19, aimless and having panic attacks in university bathrooms.

These little poems helped me to heal, to learn, and to grow.

I have divided them into four sections: Fire, Water, Earth, and Air. I often feel as though our emotions are much like the elements - a little wild and textured.

All I hope is that you find something in these words that tugs at you a little, or makes you feel less alone.

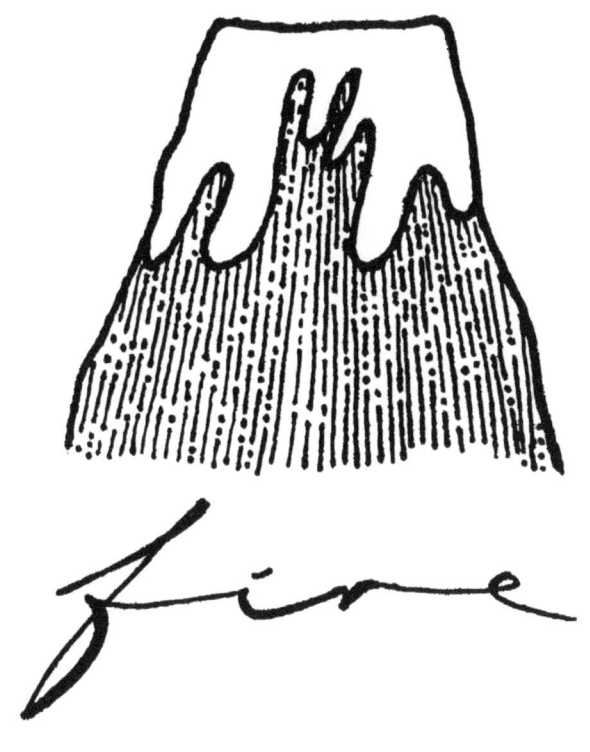

A knife edge, prickling warmth beneath your skin, anger that spits and seethes, emotion untethered.

This Feeling has Fangs and a Heartbeat

You compliment us with
you're not like other girls
as if every single individual
that identifies as female on this planet
is moulded from the same clay
with the same hands,
and hardened in the same kiln.
As if we should flutter and smile
and accept it as the highest form of flattery
to be unlike *them*
to be separate from *them*.
This is not a competition
girl is not a dirty word
they are my sisters
my friends
my supporters
the fingers that I hold when I can't breathe.
So take back your 'compliment'
no matter how kindly it was meant.
We're not here to be compared
to be flattered for diverging
from your personal idea of *norm*.
Stop bulking us together in the same goddamn
idea of *girl* when that single word
encompasses more than you
can comprehend.

GIRL IS NOT A DIRTY WORD

This anger is something alive.
It is hot and breathless,
and made of frayed electrical cables,
bruised thunderclouds,
and screaming winds.
This anger wants to split skin,
dislodge teeth and separate itself
into an entity of its own.
This anger doesn't want to wait
for the water to cool or
the waves to settle into a simmer.
I have never felt this before,
this burning, writhing, spitting
anger toward another
human being.
If you can even be called that anymore.

TO THE BOY WHO THOUGHT HE COULD TAKE WHAT WASN'T HIS

This Feeling has Fangs and a Heartbeat

When you pushed your hands beneath her jumper,
they said *boys will be boys*.
When I was too drunk to see and you let
your hands roam my body like a playground,
they said, *he was drunk*.
When you promised to sleep on the floor
and she woke up to you stealing her space,
they just shrugged it off
like swatting at a stray mosquito.
Because you were goofy and funny,
and everyone's friend.
When she passed out in your bed,
unconscious, uncomprehending,
trusting,
and she woke up feeling strange and sore,
she dared to ask you, *did I say yes?*
You smiled like it was a victory
snatched from the clutches of the enemy
and said *well you didn't say no*.

TO THE BOY WHO TOOK WHAT WASN'T HIS

Cassie Mutch

The impossibility of it
is only impossible because it doesn't fit
into the slice of world that you have carved
out for yourself, the shape that you
live snugly inside at night
oblivious, ignorant, asleep.

The repulsiveness of it
is only repulsive because you dragged your
taste into something that is far larger
than you; the world doesn't care if
your tongue doesn't find it palatable
just *don't eat it.*

The wrongness of it
is only wrong because you have decided
that your perception of right is universal,
and anything that falls outside the border
is *wrong, impossible, repulsive.*

This Feeling has Fangs and a Heartbeat

You shiver and cringe and wince
and screw up your mouth as though
you've swallowed something sour
when it is just your own prejudices
that taste so tart on your tongue.
The realisation that love may manifest
differently to your own is only repellent
because you have allowed yourself to
get stuck and stagnate in
a swamp of your own ignorance
while the world evolves and grows
and learns and embraces
around you.

TO THE NO VOTERS

A voice on the cusp of consciousness
that listens carefully to your conversations
waiting to slip sediment into open sores
to confirm the fears that eat away
at your fragile, shivering confidence.
It whispers a chant that builds
to a crescendo:
stupid
selfish
slow.
It swallows your shame and spits
it back at your face:
lazy
loathsome
lonely.
If only it were a stranger you could shun,
not a section of your own soul
more than willing to sabotage
itself for the satisfaction
of watching a wound
weep.

MONSTER

This Feeling has Fangs and a Heartbeat

I am an oil slick
and you keep taking the corners
too quick.
I tried to warn you,
but you thought I was
just sea-sick
from an ocean of over-thinking
or the can of salt-water
I'd been drinking.
I am an oil slick
and you ignored the yellow
warning signs
and took the corner
far too quick.

ROAD ACCIDENT

A girl in a waiting room
doesn't seem so obscure,
but if you knew what her mind
has made her endure
you would consider it
more of a feat.
Perhaps you would offer her
an encouraging smile
or even your seat.

A girl in a waiting room
with anxiety is like a
deer knowingly entering a
lion's den.
The lion in the den may have teeth
but a doctor has a prescription pad,
with a pen and his bias
underneath.

A girl in a waiting room
is holding her breath.
Her body is screaming out
to her in distress.
But he brushes off her worry
and ignores her doubt.
He is in a hurry and
she is simply
an overweight teen
with a mild case of stress
having a bit of a freak out.

A GIRL IN A WAITING ROOM

This Feeling has Fangs and a Heartbeat

You sit beside me, and I curl my fingers into fists so hard that my nails bite bloody crescent-moons into the skin of my palms. I avert my eyes to the ground and try to pretend that I am absorbed, by my phone, by the sky, by my melting lip balm. You pretend that you cannot see. You pretend that you cannot see how my shoulders curve inwards like I am preparing to defend a castle from an armed threat. There are spare seats scattered like open blooms, yet you act as though the one beside me has been specifically set for you. An open invitation to suggestively sit beside a girl who could rival your daughter in age. You tell me I look like a girl you once dated and when you ask me my name you wield it like it is something to be claimed and kept. I answer in monosyllables and noncommittal noises and swallow the sour sting of shame. You sit beside me and I want to slip out of my skin. I am thinking of what on me can be weaponised; keys, fingernails, perhaps a bobby pin. When you leave, you tell me it was a pleasure. I am left still considering what might have been my best defensive measure.

NIGHTMARES ON PUBLIC TRANSPORT

This Feeling has Fangs and a Heartbeat

You do not need a cape or
a bandana with eyeholes
cut out with your mum's
craft scissors
to convince yourself
that you are a heroine.
You just need yourself,
the skin you were born wearing,
the spirit that has always lived
inside you,
and acceptance,
determination,
and trust
in yourself.

WONDER WOMAN PART 1

Your words are honey coated
but I only get the bitter aftertaste,
sore teeth,
and the stomach-ache
from swallowing too many sweets
that only served to rot
my teeth.
Instead of an occasional treat
I get only cramps, and a mouthful
of deceit in the remnants
that you tried so hard
to cheat by coating them in a shell of
sugared candy that you knew
I'd not hesitate to
eat.

SLIMY

This Feeling has Fangs and a Heartbeat

This doubt isn't yours.
This doubt is second-hand,
ill-fitting, and borrowed from the closet
of someone who held their own doubt
in the centre of their chest,
clutched close in an unconscious grasp.

This doubt is manufactured
by sharp suits and copper coins
sold to you in pretty packaging
that promised perfection and improvement
and an acquirement of something
you didn't even know you wanted
to start with.

This doubt has a collar that itches,
but you've worn it for so long that
you've started to believe that it has lived
in your closet this entire time,
taking up space beside your
favourite jeans.

But it hasn't.
It has only made a home out of your trust
and you can slip out of it and return it with
the tags still attached.
You can spit it back out at their feet
like a mouthful of something sour.
This doubt isn't yours,
and you don't have to be polite
about sending it back.

THIS DOUBT ISN'T YOURS

I tried to send you a smoke signal
in hopes that you would see it
before my tongue turned to ash
and my skin melted like wax
from a candlestick.
Before my bones glowed like embers,
and my hair became a flame.
I thought perhaps by risking incineration
I would alter something inside you,
melt your disinterest
and warm the cool touch of your gaze.
I did not anticipate
that you would be too late
to stop the fire from devouring
me in my entirety.
When you arrived, the air was
thick with smoke
but I was only ash
beneath your feet.

INFERNO

This Feeling has Fangs and a Heartbeat

Don't be afraid to remind them
that you have teeth and
torn fingernails
and a voice that has been
too long tethered
and is more than
capable of
revolt and revolution.

WEAPONS AGAINST THE WORLD

Cassie Mutch

My emotions meet my indecisiveness
like a blade in a whetstone,
sharpening and weaponising
into something capable of
grievous harm.
It is my best weapon,
this unintentional
untethered emotion.

EMOTIONAL BLADE

This Feeling has Fangs and a Heartbeat

Around some people I feel edged,
and rough, and mouthy.
I am sandpaper sloughing at skin,
a serrated knife-edge sawing
through the shell.
But with others
I am the skin,
being worn away
raw, soft, silent
erosive,
and it's as though the other me,
the one that contains
something explosive,
is trapped in shadow,
inaccessible
and cowed.
And I am afraid that one day
I will be all skin
and no edge.

TWO-FACED

"Boys will be boys."
How about boys will be held accountable
for their actions just like everyone else?
How about not justifying violence
by encouraging it as a natural part of masculine
        growth?
How about boys learning that it is wrong
to touch someone without their consent,
to take what isn't theirs,
to harm someone because they are different.
Rather than letting them think
that they are exempt, that it is okay,
that it is all just part of being a boy.
Because when they get older,
and they take something vital,
that they never had the right to touch,
it is too late for excuses
and justifications.

TELL IT TO THE GIRL WHO LOST SOMETHING

This Feeling has Fangs and a Heartbeat

You either take up too much space;
a laugh too loud, chatter too constant,
a body with too many curves,
a mouth with too many teeth,
or not enough;
you don't flirt back, you don't find their jokes funny,
your knees are too bony, your voice just a whisper.
You try to squeeze into a box with a lid,
but your elbows don't bend that way,
you can't find enough air,
and there is a pressure in your head
like a balloon being blown up
by the person closing the lid.

SQUASHED

Cassie Mutch

They hang from car windows;
lanky limbed with wide grins,
they recline on park benches;
low jeans and phone screens.
Superficially non-threatening,
wide peaked hats that could not be
less menacing.
You'd pass them without a glance
if you had the chance, but there's
something about your walk that
halts their chattering talk.

Their eyes catch on your hemline,
and trip onto your skin
with eyes almost canine.
These laughing boys have spotted
prey: a woman alone.
Their method of assault is auditory:
piercing wolf-whistles
and pursed lips,
wet kissing noises
and the occasional
c'mon love! don't be like that!

This Feeling has Fangs and a Heartbeat

When you tell of your encounter
you are greeted with chuckles
and shoulder shrugs.
It's all harmless fun and
they are just wolf pups
playing a silly game.
What they don't say is that
they are indeed wolf pups
but this game is one they will
continue to play with their prey
until the game turns into
a hunt.

PREDATOR

Things women must be good at:
closing our mouths even when
every cell in our bodies
is bubbling with sound,
smiling politely when it is
anger that wants to take
to the battle ground,
scalding our skin
scrubbing out blood stains
from white,
gritting teeth against
cramps and pretending
the pain isn't akin to
being in a fist fight.
We must be good at squeezing
into carefully crafted cages
designed to please the eye
and contain those who
dare to dream of taking
to an alternate
sky.

CAREFULLY CRAFTED CAGES

This Feeling has Fangs and a Heartbeat

The monsters in fairy tales tend to
have forked tongues and fangs
and skin made from scales.
But what of the men
hunkered down in their homes
selling their daughters
to any strange man perched on a throne?

The monsters in fairy tales
devour children alive and set fire
to villages just to watch something burn.
But what of world leaders who
write laws that strip girls of
their right to learn?

The monsters in fairy tales
are painted as primitive
against man and his superiority.
But what of the lion on the run
from a man wielding a gun?
And why are predators who
stalk women down dark streets
allowed to continue on
their terror sprees?
This violence is often brushed off
because that man is someone's son
and isn't that just boys
having a bit of fun?

IN DEFENCE OF FANGS

This Feeling has Fangs and a Heartbeat

I'm sorry I wounded you with my words
and my silence both.
But you left me bloody as well
and at least I claimed responsibility
for wielding the blade,
whereas you wiped your fingerprints
clean from the handle,
eliminating any evidence of yourself
from the scene.
Sometimes my own memories
deceive me and my shadow
starts to convince me that all the pain was
self-inflicted after all
and that the guilt was all mine
because you were always so good
with your words,
so deft with planting the dagger
to compromise me
even for petty crimes.
I didn't realise that the battlements
I was building were to protect me
not from enemy soldiers
but from those
crouching behind my own
walls.

FRIENDSHIP HURTS TOO

This Feeling has Fangs and a Heartbeat

Home has a hole in it
and there is something festering
in the space left behind
and I'm afraid it might be
something within my own mind.
You cannot cram a space full
of junk in the hopes that
what was taken will feel less
like it was torn out without
first being cauterised.

Home has a hole in it
and I am afraid the infection
may have spread through my veins
and tangled itself amongst
my nerves in a place too
difficult for doctors to
operate on.

Home has a hole in it
and don't they always warn you
to prepare for the worst?
To take precautions against a world
that has grown cold toward
human hands and all the destruction
we have wreaked on its soil.

Home has a hole in it
and I am afraid it will never recover
from this loss of life, this loss
like a limb being torn from
a socket.

HOME HAS A HOLE IN IT

Feather-down feelings, tear tracks and tenuous connections, vulnerability, ebb and flow.

This feeling has fangs
and a heartbeat,
and I'm scared it will rip me
to shreds.

This feeling has hands
and body-heat,
and I'm scared it'll curl up with me
in bed.

FANGED FEELINGS

I don armour moulded from
teeth and dimples and lips turned
up at the corners.
The edges are honed by
laughter, lightness, and
practiced positivity.
I make sure the edges overlap,
to fit my whole body,
to encapsulate every surface,
and mask any dents or damages.
I check for gaps in the mirror,
although I think it can sense my lie,
so I don't look too closely
at the eyes peering back at me.

Sometimes it doesn't fit right,
this armour carefully fashioned,
and it leaves holes and openings
for honesty to leak out like tar.

DAILY BATTLEFIELD

This Feeling has Fangs and a Heartbeat

Sometimes I fall asleep,
with one arm across my body,
fingers hooked around my shoulder
in an embrace,
and I find that
it's a small mercy,
to let yourself be loved by you,
without waiting for the justification,
from another person's mouth.
Maybe it is a learned loneliness
to curl up in your own arms,
but it is a gentle kind of lonely,
the kind I would happily invite to
stay.

LONELINESS WARMED UP

Your anxiety is the kraken, and you are a ship.
Sometimes the ocean is languid,
the workers move as a cohesive unit,
and your compass needle finds north easily.
But the kraken recognises your ship now,
and it lingers in the dark hungry waters,
waiting.
Sometimes you can evade it,
you breathe a lungful of air into the sails,
and you have time to slip away.
But other times you are unprepared for an assault;
the skies are clear,
the waves kiss gently against the prow,
and then it is upon you,
threading tentacles through the wooden foundations,
snapping poles, and crushing scurrying deck-hands.
You do not have enough time to sketch an escape
        route,
or to send a desperate distress signal.
It is wrapping itself around you,
lovingly suffocating, and it is tugging you
under the waves, where the sun starts to dim,
and inky darkness reigns.

WAR AT SEA PART 1

This Feeling has Fangs and a Heartbeat

Your anxiety is the kraken and people call it myth.
They say that it was conjured up by your mind;
an imaginary, fickle thing,
that is simply a sea creature
that story exaggerated beyond recognition.
They call your distress an over-reaction
and liken it to just a niggling fear,
and a handful of nerves.
And even when it is upon you,
tentacles tightening on your torso,
stealing your breath and logical thought,
they still do not believe in its existence.
They do not see the waters rising over your head,
because they keep their eyes on the opposite horizon,
searching for distraction in the clouds.
Often the Kraken must be dispatched
with your own bare hands,
your own stuttering pulse, and your own strength,
because those who have not encountered it,
will often avert their eyes,
toward a prettier horizon that is easier
to swallow.

WAR AT SEA PART 2

This Feeling has Fangs and a Heartbeat

It is
clumsy.
A winged heart
taking flight within my rib cage,
a laugh climbing from my lips,
bursting out unceremoniously,
ungracefully, and a little unexpectedly.
This feeling has cobwebs and dust
and needs an instruction manual
to help decipher if it is one to trust.
It is a sepia memory of high-school days
when affection came easy,
crushes frequent, obvious, and always.
I do not know how to handle it,
nor how to wear it skilfully,
or with elegance and ease.
It is a dress one size too small,
that squeezes and catches on skin.
I would like to embrace it but
I do not like the itch
or how my thoughts end up with a glitch.
I think I will relegate it to the bin,
so that I can once again understand my skin,
and not feel the need for a safety pin.

SYMPTOMS OF ACCIDENTALLY FEELING THINGS

This Feeling has Fangs and a Heartbeat

It is safer behind here,
this mask made of clay
and careful consideration.
Without it, there is a chance
someone might glimpse that
the light is practiced,
the teeth are clenched,
and the smile conjured from a copy.

COSTUME PARTY

You're running down the street, hair buried in a cowl; did no one tell you to watch for that which howls? You're treading in puddles that you barely notice, even though your shoes are damp. Damp air, damp skin, and now, damp shoes with scuffed edges and worn soles. You're willing your body to move faster, but wouldn't someone be more likely to spot a girl who runs? *Slower, slower,* you think. Someone calls something that sounds like twirl or curl or girl. You try to distract yourself with thoughts of chili con carne on Friday nights and how your mum makes sure to simmer the pot for exactly three and a half minutes. If she were here she would tell you to unclench your fists. *You are not something to be crushed underfoot, you do not owe them anything, not even your anger.* Your feet quicken and you whisper, *slower, slower.* There are shops up ahead that do late night pizza deliveries and 2-for-1 noodle boxes and you know that there will be families there with children slurping soft drinks. You want to run there but you don't. They will spot a girl who runs. Someone wolf-whistles and you flinch as if the whistle has sliced through your skin. They call to you in voices tinged with alcohol and arrogance, *hey, girl!* You want to scream that your existence is not a smoke signal that summons them. You want to scream but you don't. They will skin a girl who screams. Your hair is buried in a cowl and beside you they howl.

GIRL

This Feeling has Fangs and a Heartbeat

Someone is tap dancing
on your temple,
blowing a trombone inside your skull,
playing a drum solo in place of your heartbeat,
using your ribs as guitar strings.

The instructor has lost his place,
and the rhythm has gone.
Somewhere some part of you
is trying to regain order,
but it cannot be heard over the
cacophony,
and the chaos
of spilled chords and
neglected notes.

ORCHESTRA

Cassie Mutch

You're told that they like softness;
of skin, of voice, of opinion,
but not of body.
You use sandpaper to dull your edges,
and clippers to trim the thorns
that grow inky black and poisonous
from somewhere beneath
your skin.
But you've spent too long smothering
the softness and cooking it until it
has a crust that no knives
can perforate
that you can no longer find where
the scab ends and new skin
begins.
But they who demand softness;
isn't it them who turned up
the dial on the oven
in the first place?

450 DEGREES FAHRENHEIT

This Feeling has Fangs and a Heartbeat

My body is a city of sharp corners,
of curving, chaotic streets,
of messy, litter-strewn alleys.
A city that has been stretched thin
and filled to the brim
with thoughts and opinions
that don't belong to it,
nor should belong to it.

I am trying to make it my own,
this vessel moulded by hands both
my own and not.
I am trying to teach myself to
love this city that is only now
learning where it sits on the map,
learning how to unravel the winding roads,
within its own
belly.

MUSINGS ON BODY

In my dreams, you are haloed
in softness
and my hand reaches
unconsciously for yours.
In the waking,
my doubt wears your skin
like a warning
and I cringe from your reaching
fingers.

A SORT OF APOLOGY POEM

This Feeling has Fangs and a Heartbeat

I would choose flames
and prickling skin
over a numbness
that would not even register
if someone lit the
biggest organ in my body
on fire.
I would choose hot
anger and a storm of tears
over a numbness
that would not even shiver
beneath a downpour
of icy rain.

I WOULD CHOOSE PAIN

On my birthday, my stress manifests into
bed sheets,
breakfast bowls,
and bitten fingernails.
On my birthday I hold my breath
for 24 hours and my lungs
feel ready to collapse,
and my muscles scream
and whine.
On my birthday, I am more
likely to cry than laugh properly
and it is not the getting older that scares me
but the things that have not changed,
the fear that resides and the ache
that persists and has become
as much a part of me as my own hands.

BIRTHDAY BLUES

This Feeling has Fangs and a Heartbeat

Some days you are more ghost than girl
and eyes gloss over you as though you are
merely discarded scraps
left for birds to scavenge with their beaks.
You wonder if you have disappeared
without realising it,
if the world has breathed you in
and refused to spit you back out.
You're not sure if you would know,
for eyes barely seem to stick to you
even when you are boldly present.
You could wear sequins and
rich glimmering stones and still
eyes would slip over you like water
and slowly
erode
you away.

GHOST OR GIRL?

Cassie Mutch

It's so cliche to fall
for a broken boy.
To think that you can
heal someone with just
your head and your hands.
It's so easy to wait for
a broken boy to glue himself back
together enough to give you
some of the energy you expended
stemming the flow of his pain.
But in the end all you got
was blood all over your hands
and a paper-thin knife slipped
between your ribs while
you had your back turned
trying to keep pressure
on his wounds.

YOU CAN'T HEAL BROKEN BOYS WITH YOUR HANDS

This Feeling has Fangs and a Heartbeat

Someone has taken a scalpel to your sternum,
sliced a gaping smile in your skin,
and scooped your insides out with a soup spoon,
and you're not sure how you didn't feel
the searing pain of split flesh,
nor the stolen organs.
But what other explanation
is there for this hollowness?
For the echoing beneath your skin?
When you press your ear to your stomach
you can hear only static
and when you stand you feel
like a shell
that is only an echo
of the ocean.

SURGERY ROOM

Here's a confession that eats at me like a starving
        creature;
I shiver when fingers scrape along my wrist,
my limbs go loose when someone grasps my shoulder,
my face flushes warm when I can feel someone's
        breath mingle with mine,
and I'm terrified that when someone else's skin more
        than skims mine
I might disintegrate
or worse,
slip
into a state
of senselessness.

TOUCH

This Feeling has Fangs and a Heartbeat

This feeling is as fragile as insect wings:
membranous, quivering, and delicate,
and it would take only a slight breath of wind
exhaled in exclamation to knock it askew,
like a dead leaf caught in an eddying breeze.

These are the feelings I am learning to love,
the feelings that once made me feel hot,
blushing shame.
The feelings that felt too soft to clasp in my hands,
too vulnerable to nurture.
I am learning to be softer,
and to view fragility as an inevitability,
and not a negativity.

INSECT WINGS

Cassie Mutch

I am drawn to you;
moth to a struck match,
second place to the heels of first,
fingers to the icing
on a chocolate birthday cake,
north to south,
and the planets to the sun.
But when you in turn
reach out,
hands open,
soul bared,
I whirl back toward open air,
to emptiness
and safety,
leaving you with open
palms and empty
of explanations.

I AM SO FUCKING SCARED

This Feeling has Fangs and a Heartbeat

Cassie Mutch

Here's an explanation you saw coming:
it's not you, it's me.
No, please, just listen.
I think there's something wrong with me,
a glitch that can't be detected on a blood test,
a twisted wire that is too small to identify.
Listen to me,
sometimes I can't decipher my thoughts
even when they are red and tightening
in a stranglehold around my neck.
It's not you,
I can promise you that.
If I could choose someone, it would be you
over and over,
I promise you.

IT'S NOT YOU

In another world, we make dinner in a lamplit kitchen; singlet tops and shorts and skin on balmy summer evenings. We dance badly to 97.3FM pop and forget to put a timer on for the rice, which sticks like glue to the bottom of the pan. We eat off our laps and feed our dog scraps of carrot by hand and my hair curls in the humidity and you complain that I always leave you with the washing up and we bicker like grandparents and laugh too loudly at 2am and there are trips to the ice-cream store at ungodly hours and whispered arguments in petrol-stations and we would love each other with everything and more. When I'm sad I think of this imaginary world, this parallel place where we make each other happy, and where I do not doubt my feelings for you because they are a summer storm after a day of unrelenting humidity.

PARALLEL WORLD

Lonely comes out to play at 4am.
Wide awake and shiny-eyed.
Lonely wraps you up in a doona
and holds you close.
Lonely likes last night's leftovers
and echoing spaces,
but enjoys hanging out with
you at parties as well.
Lonely doesn't discriminate
and is happy to give itself freely
to whoever leaves a gap
wide enough.
Lonely likes 4am, but sometimes
visits unexpectedly in class
or when you're sharing a meal
with a friend.
Lonely has other favourites but
you are their favourite to curl
up with
at night.

LONELY'S FAVOURITE

This Feeling has Fangs and a Heartbeat

I barely have an appetite and
all I'm craving is for you to retract
your words, change your mind,
apologise profusely and come back
to me changed, settled, okay.
You can't catch people up in
your whirlwind of pain and expect
there to be no collateral damage.
I always told myself I wouldn't be
susceptible to hazel-eyed boys who
wear their pain like armour,
but here I am,
raw and sliced open, and
there you are,
letting me bleed out.

I CRAVE YOU STILL

Cassie Mutch

You see before the battle even begins,
I am already dressed for defeat,
and when you are ready for rejection
you don't bother keeping your sword drawn,
for the chance at a victory.
You just buckle your armour
raise your shield,
and brace for impact.

DRESSED FOR DEFEAT

This Feeling has Fangs and a Heartbeat

This numbness is a canvas drained of colour,
a blanket of white draped over your head,
paper spat out of a printer that has run out
of ink.

You don't know how to say that even when you are
        laughing,
you can only tell because your lips change shape,
that even when you are angry, the anger fades to grey.
The numbness only takes a back seat to tears.
Salt has an uncanny ability to erode.

EROSION

Cassie Mutch

I could uproot myself from this place,
and move across the sea,
I could throw my phone from a cliff
and live without internet,
I could be on the moon
or just in my room,
and still be thinking of you.

UPROOT

This Feeling has Fangs and a Heartbeat

I wonder if you can feel my heartbeat shivering in the
      space between us,
the vibrating tension,
because I am sure it must be something that can be felt
outside of my body,
because there is no way that my skin can contain
      something
so freaking *loud*.

SO LOUD

Cassie Mutch

When I see you my brain disconnects
like a plug yanked from a wall socket
before the switch is flicked off,
and I forget that I am a human
with hands and a mouth and
legs and skin and
my cheeks forget which gear neutral is
and suddenly the air is too taut
to breathe and my smile feels like
someone else's and
I try to laugh and it sounds like
tyres squealing on a road,
and I think you probably think
I'm deranged, or perhaps just
very strange, but it's too late
to remedy, so I'll just sit here
and hum along to some discordant
melody because if I try to speak
to you the resulting chaos will
be all I think of for the next week.

WHEN YOU'RE AWKWARD AF

This Feeling has Fangs and a Heartbeat

It's possible I misconstrued
the movement of your shoes
but surely when you stepped
the way you did
you were heading my way,
at least in my head you were
and perhaps that's where I went wrong,
daydreaming in too much detail
so that reality loses itself in the throng.

DAYDREAM

Cassie Mutch

Here's a snippet of me:
perpetually peeling lips and
a propensity to be distracted
by the movement of hips,
an inability to properly articulate and
a tendency to be a strangely inconsistent
cheapskate.

Sometimes I feel irreparably impaired,
but I am almost never unprepared
because I've played every scenario
over in my head,
so perhaps you'll understand why
it is that I've already packed
my bags and
fled.

SELF-PORTRAIT

This Feeling has Fangs and a Heartbeat

Perpetual ponytail and
a loose, lazy grin.
I see in you in snapshots:
curled, cosy, and content
with a cup of tea and my
hand clasped in yours;
laughing loudly at
something ludicrous,
your mouth wide and uninhibited;
sleepy, soft, and centred
at night making a bed for two;
perched on the kitchen counter,
snacking on corn chips
and savouring the scent of
simmering curry.
I keep these in my pockets,
potential memories,
unlikely moments.
I'm still not sure whether imagining
them makes me feel more
or less
alone.

CRUSH

Giving my feelings to you spreads my sanity sparsely,
and gives the reigns over to my adamant anxiety
who happily helps to hinder any progress
I may have previously made.
Having you in my head renders the rest of me
restless and ridiculous and running wild.
You barely beseech me with a brief glance
and I collapse in a cascade of crumbling corners
and eroded edges.

SPARSE SANITY

This Feeling has Fangs and a Heartbeat

There is more than one me
living in my mind,
taking root in my soul.
They are split
isolated
and at war.
They sometimes come to terms,
make nice, and share space
in an almost state of equilibrium.
But mostly they want to overcome
each other,
to seize the stage
and displace the other from
their precarious podium.

I am ashamedly biased,
I too want to smother the
me that is too numb to laugh
and too heavy to lift my eyelids.
But it lives inside too, it has a
place set at the table and a seat with its name.
You see I left the doors wide open for it,
practically invited it inside,
so how can I now close the doors
in its face?

A PLACE AT THE TABLE

Cassie Mutch

Bus stop, 12:20am.
Every sound makes me flinch:
a can skittering across bitumen,
an old car indicating right,
wind shuffling a handful of leaves
in the sky above my head.
My shoulders are barricades,
my fingers curled fists.
My keys are claws extended
between my knuckles,
my bus card a knife
in my palm.
Tears lodged in my throat
and the corners of my eyes,
and I'm remembering why I'm never
up at this hour of silence
where any noise is an echo,
a gunshot, a warning.
All my feelings congregate
and float to the surface together
blocking my windpipe
and fogging my thoughts.

This Feeling has Fangs and a Heartbeat

My body feels both like a husk,
exhausted and drained dry,
and a water balloon,
taut and on the brink of a flood,
and I can't stop thinking about
my inability to be a normal,
functioning human
when it really matters
and also
what if my bus
doesn't
come?

WHAT IF MY BUS DOESN'T COME?

Cassie Mutch

I see you in the curve of my cheeks
and the upturned slope of my nose.
I hear you when a bad joke lands on my tongue,
and when my stubbornness shows.
Thank you for showing me that
tears don't tend toward gender,
that spices shouldn't be measured
by spoons but by taste instead,
that compassion toward animals
is not up for contention,
and that there is always time
to stop for sunsets.

DAD

This Feeling has Fangs and a Heartbeat

My car always smells like dog hair
and dirty soccer boots
and crushed grass
and the radio will be playing 97.3FM
and sometimes the engine hiccups
going up hills and I guess I
just need you to know that
I am like my car in that I
am always snuggling dogs and
getting messy and I like bad karaoke
music and singing too loudly
and I don't function well under pressure
or in general really and I breakdown
unexpectedly and frequently and
I thought this should all be included
in the manual before you agree
to anything that you might
regret.

ADVANCED APOLOGY

Cassie Mutch

In another world my thoughts
don't eat me from the inside out
and I don't exist just to
bandage your wounds
while mine seep and scab
with infection running rife.

In this world I am sure of myself
and I don't hesitate before picking
up the phone to make a risky call
or to demand clarity from the mouth
of a man who speaks in riddles.

In this world I stop forgiving you.
I listen to my gut which is screaming
at me to run away as fast as I can
before I compromise even more of myself
to cater to your every whim.

In this world I remember how to
look after myself again.
I relearn my old routines,
pick up pilates and yoga and poetry.
I get out of bed even when
I want to curl up and drown in tears.
I stop prioritising you and slowly
rebuild this body into something
resilient with only surface scratches
instead of a river of fragmented bones.

This Feeling has Fangs and a Heartbeat

In this world I forgive you for your chaos
but I don't let this empathy
keep me tethered to you.
I walk away even when I want
to stay and give everything to you.
I walk away and I am alive again.

IN THIS WORLD I AM ALIVE

The lack of.
The emptiness.
A lonely void.
A space that was once
filled by something
that brought only joy,
laughter and love.

The habits that must be changed,
the unconscious movements
that must be unlearned.

It is a space devoid of
a fundamental feeling,
one that once felt like home
and now feels like a star that
has eaten itself into
nothingness.

GRIEF IS AN EMPTY SPACE

This Feeling has Fangs and a Heartbeat

This feeling has fissures of hope
disguised as something attainable,
appealing and possible.
This feeling beckons me close
to the edge of the ravine
with a breathy whisper that dusts
a disguise of stability over a
surface of loose stones.
This climb is made for those with
ropes and pulleys and harnesses,
not a girl staggering barefoot,
blind with desire.
These fissures are open mouths
crowded with jagged rocks
that hide in wait for anybody stupid
enough to peek inside the gaping
darkness, expecting to see something
other than a row full of
hungry, waiting
mouths.

FISSURES

Cassie Mutch

I am a court fool
and you are a traveller
passing through.
With my every movement
the bells attached to my limbs
jingle and shriek.
You cannot look away from
a fool acting the freak.
Would you take me more
seriously if I were dressed in
something a little more bleak?
Or if I didn't stumble every time
I tried to speak?
Even out of costume,
the idiocy manages to leak
and my every move becomes
a question of just how much
havoc my mind can wreak.

THE FOOL

This Feeling has Fangs and a Heartbeat

This world builds boys with armour
instead of skin.
With the carved teeth of
carnivores when their mouths are not
made to house fangs.
This world tells boys to keep their
emotions contained within chests
made of both flesh and wood,
padlocked with jaws and steel.
This world builds boys with bones
that can break but are not allowed to.
So, when something splinters it is
hidden and endured
and when the bone finally begins to heal
it sets in the wrong place.
And when all the bones in a body
have been melted into shapes not made
to be contained by soft human skin,
what emerges from the flesh
is no longer a boy
but a monster.

BOYS BUILT BY THE PATRIARCHY

Cassie Mutch

I am holding my breath for you,
withholding my desire for you,
consoling my inevitable grief about you,
moulding my world around you,
and scolding my brain for its inability
to dream about anything other than
you.

I WISH I COULD STOP WRITING ABOUT YOU

This Feeling has Fangs and a Heartbeat

Your name is a dagger and
I am a body of flesh
without an army to defend it.

Your smile is a staircase and I
didn't look to see if the pavement
was flat before I took a step
forward.

Your hands are smoke and I
let myself be mesmerised
and now I can't seem to catch
my breath.

Your words are in weepy handwriting
and I left my glasses discarded
face-down on my bedside table.

YOU MAKE MY BRAIN MALFUNCTION

With my sandpaper skin
and forked tongue,
am I creature you cannot
abide?
If I were to catch your eye
would your skin
shiver in revulsion
at the sight of my peeling hide?
My lower lip uncurls
to reveal a row of broken
teeth and if you peel back
my flesh you may find
blackened blood beneath
because I do not think I
was made for this world
and if you were to delve a little
deeper you may find that
my very personality is something
that must be unfurled
clumsily, in an attempt to be patriotic,
to plead a semblance of belonging
in a space that
isn't my own
silence.

ALIEN

This Feeling has Fangs and a Heartbeat

My skin is eggshell thin
and if you were to look closely
you would see the spider-thin
veins threaded within.
I wear my words like weapons
hooked onto my hip.
It would only take the slightest
change in the shape of your lip
to shatter this skin into fragments
sharp enough to shred any
remaining confidence into filaments.
I spent my life fitting myself into
a costume made of wood
but the weather ate the ground
where I stood
and I was left with this eggshell skin
and a fear of words and
anything that makes my
armour feel thin.

EGGSHELL SKIN

I unearthed this drumbeat beneath my skin,
a chant carved so carefully I almost missed
it when I traced my fingers over ridges
like goosebumps beneath the surface.

This drumbeat is so constant it has become
a steady buzz that blends in with my breath,
each inhalation hiding the rhythm.

This   is   not   good   enough

I stumbled across it when I paused to
properly listen without realising what
it was that I was keeping an ear out for.

The drumbeat has become the rhythm my
mind moves to, the beat my body unconsciously
convenes with before making decisions.

You   are   not   good   enough

How do you destabilise something so inherent,
so intertwined with each nerve in your body?
How do you consciously unlearn a habit
that is so unconsciously ingrained?

ME VS MY BRAIN

This Feeling has Fangs and a Heartbeat

I keep seeing you in cigarette butts
and my favourite jeans that you loved so much.
I keep hearing you when a diesel
car drives down my street
and in the album I played on repeat
when you and I were just on the cusp
of being something.
I can smell you when I wear essential oils
on my wrist and when someone
is smoking weed.
I feel you when I am in my empty bed
and my insides feel so hollow
I can barely breathe and I just want to
feel your fingertips tracing the curve
of my cheekbone
so gently,
like my face was something you were
trying to keep in your memory forever.
Do you still see my face
or have you tucked it away beside
everything else you kept trying
so hard to forget?

I KEEP SEEING YOU

Crescent moons and cosy rooms, sunlight kissing collarbones, ease, trees that offer reprieve and saltwater seas.

This Feeling has Fangs and a Heartbeat

Bedroom, 6am:
summer.
Sunlight like syrup
slipping through the gaps
between curtains, corners
and the kaleidoscope of thoughts
refracting in patterns over
the skin of the wall and the skin
stretched over your bones.
The world feels both sparse and
sprawling, both small and stuffed
with possibility and potential,
and you need only to open
your palms, your eyes, and that
part of your mind that closes
automatically in the face of
the unfamiliar, the new, and
the scary.
Your world has not had time
to settle and wake,
to remember the burdens of
yesterday.
There is only today
and today is bathed in
      syrup
and blind to hesitation.
Today is only yes
yes
yes.

TODAY

This autumn air is cool, a little crisp,
it nips at exposed ankles and fingertips.
I want to bottle it for summertime,
in a jar that used to house honey,
or perhaps raspberry jam with pips.
This autumn sky is a blue softening to grey,
pastel colours painted by a careful hand;
a backdrop for the trees and their gentle sway.

Autumn in Australia is a mouthful of relief,
from a bottle promising to be heat's thief.
It is rolled up jeans and tops with sleeves,
it is the allure of the warm morning sun,
instead of reclining in an air-conditioned room for
        fun.
It is a feeling I try to take in sips,
lest winter steals it away too soon,
this soft season with kind hands,
and its tender introduction to June.

SWEET AUTUMN

This Feeling has Fangs and a Heartbeat

Cassie Mutch

Cluttered, clumsy, cosy rooms,
with loud, dirty-pawed pups,
always nosing palms and licking fingers,
and the hum of bees seeking pollen
in a slightly over-grown garden,
and a kettle always about to boil,
for a cuppa.
Sometimes the air smells of
baking bread, or simmering curry,
or smoke from fires in the hills.
It is always warm, even in the chill,
even when my fingers are icy,
and my nose cold to touch.
Even when someone is yelling,
or upset, or saying something that
hurts.
It is always warm,
and the kettle is always about
to boil.

HOME

This Feeling has Fangs and a Heartbeat

Brush stroke clouds,
painted by a gentle hand.
Purple flowers wreathed
in sleepy golden sunlight.
Shards of sun rays spilling
through branches that reach
like fingers toward the soft lilac sky.
The air is crisp and kisses at
the strip of skin between my
sock and the hem of my leggings,
at my neck beneath my plait,
cooling the sweat on my skin.
For once my mind is empty,
hollowed out, and clear.
It is an empty glass tipped upside-down,
a sky cleared of thunderclouds,
a canvas before the paint splatter.

AFTERNOON ON TWO WHEELS

I crave warmth at night.
Isn't that so well worn,
so rubbed raw?
That night is for skin other than your own,
and exhalations against your ear?
Daylight is too harsh
and my flaws have fewer nooks
to hide away in,
and so after sunrise
I crave only space.
But at night I crave less
space and
more skin.

CRAVINGS

This Feeling has Fangs and a Heartbeat

Give me a sea of sunflowers,
grubby, soil-covered hands,
crescents of dirt underneath fingernails,
thorny stems that bite skin,
fallen petals on floorboards,
and angry, spiky cacti.

I would not know what to do,
with a room with no leaves,
a yard devoid of colour,
or smooth hands,
with unchipped nail-polish,
or a cacti without bite.

SEA OF SUNFLOWERS

Cassie Mutch

The plants in my garden flourish
on days when they are drenched in sunlight,
and kissed softly by summer showers.
But some days they wilt away from
the blistering sun, and flounder beneath
a vicious downpour that threatens to
drown them in their own flooding homes.
But they persist.
There are days when I do not think
that they will live to see the next sunrise,
but I awake to find them reaching up toward the rising
        sun,
their spindly brown fingers freckled with buds
like tiny sealed up seashells.
Lime shoots peek out from the ground
like small creatures emerging after a forest fire.
Plants can survive the elements and chaos
thrown at them from the sky, and the earth.
And you can survive screaming summer storms,
and days that threaten to overwhelm
as well.

PLANT POWER

This Feeling has Fangs and a Heartbeat

An overcast Sunday in October;
sky the colour of a pale moon waning,
and a horizon of weak earl grey tea.
Leaves tangle in a breeze
that is just a whisper of a winter long past.
The air smells like the promise of rain,
and sporadic raindrops tap on the tin roof;
a prelude to the deluge sweeping in
from the West.
I am thinking of an essay that needs writing,
and how many shifts I need to do to afford
that fantasy of a trip to Iceland.
I am thinking that loneliness can
be both the colour of an ocean drop-off,
dark, remote, fathomless,
and of the watery remnants of forgotten tea,
anaemic, familiar, depthless,
and how they too, can coexist
within you.

THE FIRST SUNDAY IN OCTOBER

Cassie Mutch

There's a yawning space inside me,
that can only be filled
by buttery warm sunlight,
the breeze that skips off salty waves,
mountains that smudge blue across the horizon,
ivy that climbs window frames,
storms that bruise skylines and split the night,
and everything leafy,
and wild,
and *alive*.

LOVE LETTER TO THE EARTH

This Feeling has Fangs and a Heartbeat

Bougainvillea flowers scatter
pearl pink and dusk red,
and summer has started to
kiss the world before I awake,
and nights no longer bring shivers
and long-sleeves,
and there's a hopefulness in this warmth,
and a gentleness that I was blind
to before, and I want,
more than anything,
for this heat to ignite something
beneath my skin,
to eke out the fear and the loneliness
and everything that is stopping me
from being and seeing and breathing more,
and so I wrap arms around it,
and press the warmth against my skin
even when it singes my hair and
kisses red angry welts onto my body,
even then
I hold it close.

CATHARSIS

The days stretch like elastic,
pliant and hazy and warm,
and mangoes the colour of
a sleepy sunrise weigh down the branches
until the trees look as though they are
reaching toward the earth for an embrace.
Days are spent poolside, beachside,
anywhere that offers a reprieve in the form
of cool water and saturated hair.
Your fingers wrinkle from too much
exposure to water, and the sun
crisps your skin a blushing pink
and you try not to think of your age
of how you should be doing more,
learning more, experiencing more.
You bury your worries in grains of sand,
sticky melting ice cream
and the hopes that summer will swallow
everything that you fear
whole.

SUMMER IGNORANCE

This Feeling has Fangs and a Heartbeat

I find stillness nooks;
plant pots and paint brushes,
puppy paws and plush pillows.
I can breathe easier in these
tiny fragments,
in the very corners of moments,
the ordinary and the unassuming.
These nooks are the brakes
on a vehicle that struggles to
slow, and sightsee, to
breathe and find balance.
I often neglect the oil,
and leave the fuel light until
it is choking and gasping
and then re-fill it until
it almost spits back out
the top,
but these nooks offer ease
and soothe a restlessness
that is determined to stay.

STILLNESS

Cassie Mutch

Summer comes in waves;
at first you can no longer go barefoot on bitumen
and the ocean feels less like it'll turn you blue.
Storm clouds gather more frequently
and the heat feels damp and heavy,
as though it is keeping a promise from you.

Summer comes in waves;
and at first you fight it
and keep your winter drawer full.
When rain gives way to a cool
breeze you slip on a jacket
as if you can manifest the cold
back into being.

Summer comes in waves;
and you and the heat get along
better than you used to.

Summer used to be all sweat
and vulnerable skin and
an attempt to hide your thighs.
But now when summer arrives, your skin
glows and flowers bloom and thrive,
and you soak in the ocean and
let the sun place kisses on your shoulders.

SUMMER SKIN

This Feeling has Fangs and a Heartbeat

I wrote to you in the Summer,
on a night made of swollen
storm-clouds and
air that felt dense enough to slice.
I know that you didn't receive
my mail
and so the ink on the page
ran in bruised rivulets
of unsaid thoughts.

DELAYED MAIL

Medusa was misunderstood,
and who can blame the sirens of the sea
for taking what they needed to sustain
their innate needs?
Medusa used the only weapon
at her disposal to destroy men who thought
to take what wasn't theirs, and maybe
she didn't always want to destroy,
but those who came for her always carried cruelty
like a shield,
and she had no choice but to defend herself
against prejudice and male fear toward
a being that they could not best,
a woman who was more terrifying than
their edged blades could ever be.
The sirens of the sea were always painted wickedly,
but weren't they just creatures seeking prey?
Why is a woman who can defeat a man drawn so
crudely by a biased hand?

MYTH

This Feeling has Fangs and a Heartbeat

I am a homebody deep into my bones.
I miss the colour of my walls
when I'm away
from home,
and I dream of the depression in my bed
and the soft indentation left by my head.
But if someone knocked on my door
with a ticket to the moon,
I would shut the door to my room
and pack a spare pair of shoes
into a suitcase a size too small,
and be gone before
the door has settled against the wall.

HOMEBODY ON THE MOON

I detest these late summer nights,
the air so thick and soupy with
sticky skin and sweat,
and salt on the edge of my lip,
words cramped somewhere
between my head and my tongue,
indecipherable.
I like the way the word balmy fits into my mouth
but using it would make me a liar.
I am fire, my body curled,
fingers searching for a cool reprieve.
Nightmares parallel with the feverish heat.
Should I compare thee to a summer's day?
No, Shakespeare, to a night.
Suffocating, torrid, raw, aphotic.
If I could give you a namesake it would be
summer's night.

SUMMER'S NIGHT

This Feeling has Fangs and a Heartbeat

The moon tugs on the tides and the world tilts on an axis and we exist in the middle of an expansive, endless space with exploding stars and you still don't believe in magic?

MAGIC SPELLS

Cassie Mutch

Autumn is here and I swear
I write a poem about it every year,
because it always feels like both
the start and
the end,
and as though the world is giving me
a second chance,
a moment of respite,
a chance to find me in the fray once again.

AUTUMN

This Feeling has Fangs and a Heartbeat

Cassie Mutch

I thought I was better, but I was just busy.
I thought I was better but when the bustle
slows, when a free day is conjured from thin air,
it sneaks back in.
A shadow, a spilled ink well,
a handful of a night sky void of stars.
I think it lives in my bones and only exhaustion
keeps it in bed,
because when my calendar shows some skin
I am suddenly back where I began
and even breathing feels like a mountain
that needs to be scaled.

I THOUGHT I WAS BETTER

This Feeling has Fangs and a Heartbeat

If I could distil this power you have over me
into a jar,
you could sell it for a fortune
to someone who
needs to move a mountain
or pull clouds from the air
or perhaps rewind themselves
back into just the particles
of a star.

STARDUST

Cassie Mutch

I think it's telling that when
our knowledge was barely the width
of a whisker
framed from a finite view out of our
blue-skied astrodome,
that we assumed our home
was the centre of it all.
We thought that Earth was
perched on the throne of this
expansive, unfathomable solar system,
and that the sun in all its
blistering, devastating
glory was but a rib to Earth's backbone.
And isn't that funny?
That from the beginning
we saw ourselves as worth orbiting around,
as something more than soil and stone.

This Feeling has Fangs and a Heartbeat

Doesn't it now make sense
why our world is decaying around us
while we sit perched on a power honed
from the destruction of anything that tried
to stay afloat with us at
the helm.
We have only ever known
how to be ignorant
and how to claim it all
for our own.

TUNNEL VISION

Cassie Mutch

I'll go back to drinking turmeric tea
and ginger juice.
I'll sink my teeth into cloves of garlic
and slices of lemon.
I was wondering what it would be like
to swallow an apple core whole.
I get sticky hands plucking the seeds out when
I feed leftover chunks to my dogs
because I'm afraid the cyanide might
be just enough to kill them but
I'm not afraid of the poison myself.
If it wanted to hurt me it would have
done so already when my ignorance
was still friends with it.
Maybe if I swallow an apple
core whole
something beautiful and ancient and resilient
will grow from my mouth
and from my nail beds
and the space between my knuckles.
Perhaps my skin will peel off in layers
of wrinkled bark instead of floating particles
that clog up sinks and settle on porcelain
statues and half-melted candles.
I could grow something sweeter than
split-ends and spite for what isn't
and won't be, but
could have been,
mine.

APPLE TREE

This Feeling has Fangs and a Heartbeat

My insides are reflected in the sky today.
Whipped cream clouds tinged grey by
the weight of absorbing too much
water from rivers run by strangers.
Both my tear ducts and the clouds
share a similar state;
both overdue for a downpour
and both heavier for the burden of others.
There is blue peeking through over there
but it is being swallowed slowly.
The world is cocooned in a soft cotton-ball,
a blanket of protection against
sharp edges and rough surfaces.
It is a comfort but perhaps a
claustrophobic one.
When does comfort become constrictive?
How long does it take to become a
hiding place for your pain to fester?

POEMS WRITTEN ON BUSES

This Feeling has Fangs and a Heartbeat

It has been raining for almost a week straight. At least it feels like a week. It could be closer to four days, or perhaps five but the relentless grey skies tend to play with time. I usually adore the rain, the smells it brings and the clarity that comes after. And I do this time as well. Everything is so green it is almost blinding, and it is cool enough to wear a sweater with the sleeves rolled up and it feels as though the world is giving us one last reprieve before winter concedes. I love it but it is also making me restless, though perhaps that is just life as it currently stands - brimming with possibilities, questions and the unknown. Somehow this weather, this steady trickle, feels like an in between space, an unreal space. A space where I could skip class for a week or forget to hand in an assignment or buy something I can't afford, and there would be no repercussions because, in the real world, it never happened. Usually, this weather helps me to breathe and step back but this feels more like a breath held or a question that has gone unanswered.

15 OCTOBER 2018

I am in love with the space between Winter and
        Spring;
the handover, the touch of fingertips,
the transfer of energy.
The change in the wind, the mingling of two seasons
that only have the space of a second to share a breath
before they part ways for another year.
A year that could carry with it
unforeseen disaster or unfathomable disrepair.

The philosophers say that we cannot take
the sun rising today for granted so perhaps
next year will bring with it a day without light
or a night sky that swallows the moon.
But in this moment, there is only a lull
in which there are two holding the weight
usually lifted by one
and the future seems so very far
away.

THE SPACE BETWEEN BREATHS

This Feeling has Fangs and a Heartbeat

Change, a nipping breeze, whispered beginnings and epiphanies, a breath inhaled as something and expelled anew.

This Feeling has Fangs and a Heartbeat

To breathe slower,
think softly,
chew properly,
be.
To sleep easily,
see clearly,
process properly,
still.

WISHLIST

It is okay to be stuck,
to be hovering, to be restless,
and lost.
This yearning
for forests carpeted in moss,
for car rides with the volume right up,
for stories printed on paper,
for a hand to hold,
for hot sand beneath your feet,
it will come.
It is okay to be stuck,
but only if you are willing
to pull yourself out.

NOTE TO SELF

This Feeling has Fangs and a Heartbeat

A sunburnt sky fading to pink,
lips free from hairline cracks,
summer skin,
rich hot chocolate with tendrils of steam,
this heaviness to ease,
calm, gentle thoughts,
chatter resonant and loud,
midnight movie theatres and salty popcorn,
fingers to tangle with,
a mind to rely on.

WISHLIST IN NOVEMBER 2017

I will collect your fallen eyelashes, braid them into insect wings and keep them safe for you until you need to wish for something strong enough to lift your feet from this place where you have gotten stuck and take you somewhere you can breathe again.

I will keep a stash of your favourite spicy chai tea so that whenever you visit you never have to worry about being without comfort or warmth or the simple, soft reassurance of something familiar.

I will listen even when your words are a thunderstorm thrashing at the glass windows, rattling them in their frames and threatening to shatter them into silence. I will let your tears and your writhing words be, even if the shards of glass nick my skin on their way out.

I will hold onto your hand when the world is dragging you sideways in an attempt to tug your limbs from their sockets and your mind from safety. But when you want to follow the world into the wilderness with a mouth full of hope, and eyes brimming with expectation, I will
>					let
>							you
>									go.

I WILL NEVER KEEP YOU FROM YOURSELF

Cotton-ball scattered skies,
tea cool enough to hold
in both hands,
strangers with smiles to give
for free,
rose-scented moisturiser,
books held in one hand
(without cracking spines),
strawberries,
7am sunlight.

THINGS I LOVED THIS WEEK

They don't warn you of grey;
of moments when it is neither black
nor white,
when your right could easily be
very wrong,
or when wrong could lead
to the best path,
and right only to a messy
aftermath.
They don't warn you that
grey is far more common
than light and dark
so you are unarmed and
unprepared when you meet it -
hazy, inconsistent, vicious grey
who gives you less notice
than black ever
would.

GREY

This Feeling has Fangs and a Heartbeat

Sometimes a heroine is just
a girl,
 taking a deep breath,
  climbing out of bed,
   and facing the day.

WONDER WOMAN PART 2

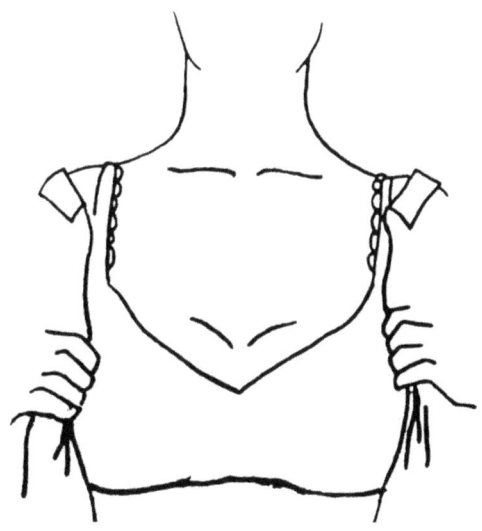

You dress as a wolf for Halloween.
You sharpen your teeth until
they are like thorns
growing from your gums.
You say *no* to hungry men
without second-guessing
yourself.
You saunter with certainty
and do not avert your eyes
from those who wish to
intimidate you
and you are not afraid to
howl and scream
when you are wronged
because their words cannot
pierce your skin.
You dress as a wolf for Halloween,
and decide to keep your
costume
on.

WOLF

This Feeling has Fangs and a Heartbeat

Cool girl keeps her cool.
Cool girl can devour a hamburger
then carve up a catwalk.
Cool girl can do cocktail and casual,
and nail both.
Cool girl is chill.
Cool girl is smart,
but lets you win.
mostly.
Cool girl can crush beer cans
and sip champagne.
Cool girl comes to the cricket,
in a jersey and cut-offs.
Cool girl never *loses it*
or acts like a *crazy bitch*.
Cool girl is uncool enough
to remain cool.

Cool girl is a figment
of unrealistic expectation,
imagination, and fetishisation.
Cool girl is a creation
from your idealised imagination.

COOL GIRL

Stillness is not just physical,
noise is not always auditory,
you can drink too much water,
being busy doesn't always
mean you are living.

EPIPHANIES

This Feeling has Fangs and a Heartbeat

The hooks they left in your
skin aren't real.
I'll tell you this again; they aren't real.
They aren't made from metal,
or steel or rusted iron,
or spare parts from your dad's workshop.
They are just hammered habit,
and a sharpened sense of
expectation and ease and everything
you ever thought that you wanted.
But you weren't created to be
sedentary and static and *same*,
and the hooks are just shadows
from a time when you were an
entirely. different. creature.
You are stubborn and stretching,
and *thriving* and you cannot be
dragged down by hooks in your
skin that are merely your nostalgia
getting comfortable in your bones.

LET THE PAST SLEEP

I promise you that this emptiness can be filled,
even if it feels as though even your very organs
have been stolen out and replaced
with echoing, endless nothingness,
that there still remains a glimmer.
I promise you,
even on days when
you are more shell than flesh,
more skeleton than skin
you will feel warm again,
and you will feel happiness,
I promise you
I promise you
I promise
you.

YOU WILL FEEL WARM AGAIN

This Feeling has Fangs and a Heartbeat

I forget what happy feels like until it crests;
engulfing me like an ocean wave breaking
salt and sand and fizzing soda on the shore.
I forget how good happy feels,
how real and tangible and giddy,
and warm and whole and kind it is.
I have reduced the word happy to a lip twitch,
a lack of sorrow, a cup half-empty,
when real happiness is a laugh that leaves lines
and a bubble that can't be squashed.
I forget that *this* happiness is worth cold fingers
and aching throats;
that shivers and brimming tear ducts are worth
fighting, understanding, and having
if it means I get to feel
this too.

FIZZING SODA

Undress your fear in the backseat of an old car, in the hazy yellow glow of a streetlamp perched on the corner of a road with a cul-de-sac. Kiss fear softly, and be gentle with your hands, for fear is shy and unused to such tenderness of touch that doesn't singe hair or leave a scar. Learn of fear's secrets and whisper your own, uttered beneath your breath, barely an exhale of air as cool as stone, mingling with the scent of worn seat covers and half-eaten takeaway Thai curry. Hold fear's hand and neglect your phone, don't let your ringtone encourage you to hurry. Let your tears have the space to carve rivers along the curve of your cheekbones, for this is honesty, alive without worry. Embrace fear like a lover, and do not avert your face from the reality you discover, and as you slip from the car, promise that you will see fear again. Weave your promises through your fingertips and do not let your palms open empty. Leave your number scrawled on the back of a grocery receipt in a weeping black sharpie pen that stains your fingers, tucked into fear's front jacket pocket; a vow wrapped like a sweet.

UNDRESS YOUR FEAR

This Feeling has Fangs and a Heartbeat

An honesty I'm too afraid share,
a feeling that feels too fragile
to bear.
One stray comment
is all it would take to shatter
this certainty that has taken root.
I coaxed water into soil that
hadn't ever borne fruit,
and it would only take a whisper of wind
to rip this green shoot from the ground.
I tried to write it down
because speaking feels too much
like truth,
but the written word can be touched,
and spoken aloud,
and so I swallow this honesty whole,
and try to pretend that this feeling
isn't so loud.

CONFESSIONS

Cassie Mutch

Inside I am lava and caramel,
longing and salt water.
At night, I reach across my queen-sized bed,
and I do not know why my fingers expect to meet
    flesh,
when they have been reaching for my whole life,
and have always found empty air.

I AM ALONE

This Feeling has Fangs and a Heartbeat

I last saw you laugh on a day by the sea,
in a car with the windows rolled down,
under clouds promising a deluge,
and sun promising pink skin.
I last saw you smile on a Monday,
from the passenger seat of my car,
on the way home
from the ocean.
I last saw you on a crowded bus,
in the window seat
with your nose in a book.
I almost said hello, but the bus stopped
and I slipped from my seat
and stepped into the crowd,
letting it swallow me up
before you could rise.

PASSENGER SEAT

If I could sketch, I would draw skylines
and singular portraits.
I would put words on paper
in perfect parallel order
without punctuation or
distracting determiners.
I would tell you how I feel without stuttering.
I would draw my emotion
in careful cursive and you wouldn't
misinterpret all that I am trying
to articulate with my mangled
words and mumbling mouth.
If I could sketch, I would draw cities
in sparkling clarity and soft hues.
I would show you how I feel without stumbling.
I would not have to pull words
from my throat using tired tweezers.
I would not have to coerce my own honesty
with promises of stability.
If I could sketch, I would be able to
make sense of my own insides before I try
to spew them
onto you.

IF I COULD SKETCH

This Feeling has Fangs and a Heartbeat

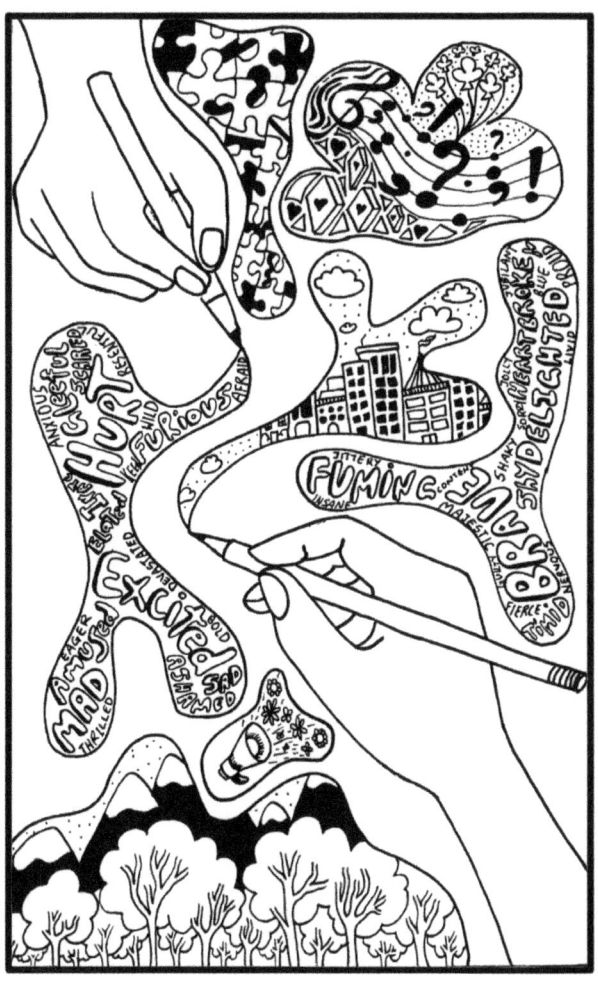

Cassie Mutch

Anger is not always noisy,
misery not always a cascade,
happiness is not always yellow,
and exhaustion is not always caused
by only getting a few hours of sleep.

TUNE IN

This Feeling has Fangs and a Heartbeat

I dream of knuckles,
of hands and of the skin
beneath your eyes.
I want to know what it feels like
to see another human as something
other than a combination of
moving pieces,
to be thrown by the
curve of their jawline
or the bitten edge of their nail,
to see a home rather than
a body of flesh.

MOVING PIECES

Lately my skin has felt less like my own and more like something borrowed. It's not an uncomfortable feeling, but more like something hopeful, like something with room to stretch out in. There are gaps that I'm still unsure of, like a sweater two sizes too big, that needs a couple of outings before you're sure of the fit. I can see the person I want to be and the person I know I can become and some days she's so close that we're almost one. Some days she's distant, beyond the reach of my fingertips and on those days, I keep my fear close so that it cannot manifest itself beyond my grasp. Because I know that each year I move forward, and each year this skin makes more sense.

GROWTH

This Feeling has Fangs and a Heartbeat

3pm is such an unromantic time.
The sun is halfway high and everyone
on the roads is rushing
and my brain won't stop trying
to squash thoughts of you in amongst
the chaos,
and in this light the hopelessness
of you and I is carved in sharp
clarity.
I only want to think about you
when the light is sleepy
and reality blurs slightly
into a place where dreams
and unrealistic yearnings
have a chance to slip from the shadows
and dance.

3PM

Cassie Mutch

This body is made from the dust of a far-off moon,
from the collision of two collapsing stars
and the broken bits of molten rock that
slipped unseen from the maelstrom in search
of something to hide away inside.
This body is more than the flesh
your lover decided against,
more than a mouth your friend
stopped wanting to listen to
and more than a canvas for the world
to throw paint onto.
This body is a phenomenon of puzzle pieces
that came together from incomprehensible,
and utterly unpredictable
chaos and it is
yours.

THIS BODY IS YOURS

When I was young, I would jerk awake at night
with pain lancing through my limbs.
I would curl my body up tight
with my knees tucked under my chin
as if the ache could be dispelled
by gritting my teeth into a forced grin.
My gran would call them growing pains,
a natural side effect of a body
in a period of growth.
My growing pains feel different now.
This ache is less about skin stretching
to accommodate muscle and bone
and more about a constant
question of what it means
to call this body,
which holds everything I am,
home.

GROWING PAINS

Cassie Mutch

A concept:
You: football jersey, converse shoes,
and hair tied on the top
of your head.
Me: loose legged pants and one of
your shirts knotted at my waist.
Our hands: loosely clasped,
palms sticky from too many strawberries
and sweating icy poles.
A thermos: wedged between our knees
filled with simmering tea
sweet enough to make our teeth
cringe.
The night sky: expansive above our heads,
speckled with constellations I wish I could
whisper in your ear.
We are ants in the midst of an avalanche,
dust on a spitting volcano,
but our world is just the space
between our fingertips and the way
our eyes find each other when
the only light is the glow of the
sun sparing a kiss for the moon.

A SKETCH FROM MY IMAGINATION

This Feeling has Fangs and a Heartbeat

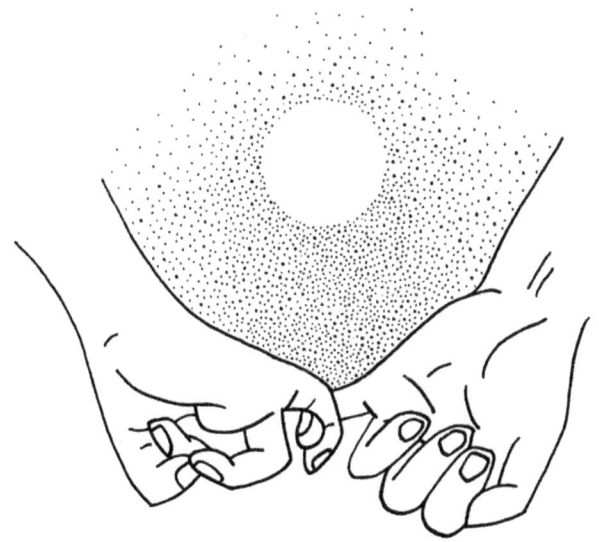

You see I thought it was a glitch.
An explanation that felt more acceptable,
but really it was always a niggling itch
that I tried to pretend wasn't perceptible
because I knew that my world may not
find it cognisable.
And I was scared that my family
would no longer find me
recognisable,
when in fact, it was I
who was struggling to recognise
myself because I was garbed in
a stranger's cape,
trying to make excuses as to why
I felt so miserable.

HAPPY PRIDE

It's like this.

In your head the worst that could happen feels paralysing. You feel swallowed whole by the very idea of it. Your chest feels as though it cannot contain the possibility of it.

When it happens, it feels worse than you ever could have imagined and for a time you barely get enough air to keep your lungs working. But then you start to breathe easier. You're not sure when the breaths start to feel less like lifting a weight above your head and more like lowering it to the ground. The pain eases so slowly that it takes weeks for you to realise that you're no longer being crushed beneath it.

And so, it goes. Your resilience is always greater than you imagine it to be, and you can weather the storms that swallow houses whole.

IT'S LIKE THIS

ACKNOWLEDGEMENTS

How do you write acknowledgements for every person who has had a hand in shaping who you are?

Rather than giving myself a panic attack trying to list every person who made this possible, I want to thank my mum and dad.

Thank you for being my number one fan(s) from the very start. Even if I was absolute trash at writing, you would still cheer from the rooftops. I'm sorry I didn't become an elite soccer player and I'm sorry if reading any of these poems hurts. Thank you for my love of words. I love you both.

Maybe if I'm lucky enough to share my words again, I'll be better at saying thank you.

ABOUT THE AUTHOR

Cassie is a writer of words and lover of nature, vegan nachos, stories, sport, and her rescue dog, Buzz. When she isn't writing about her feelings, she is working full-time as a marketing and communications professional for a non-profit.

To stay up to date with Cassie and Buzz, follow her Instagram @acuppawithcas.

ABOUT THE ARTIST

Hayley is an artist with a passion for conservation and sustainable living. She takes artistic inspiration from the wildlife and scenery around her childhood home in the Northern Territory, capturing the rugged terrain and secret oases.

Her love of the natural world comes through in her art and she enjoys highlighting the beauty of the lesser known and misunderstood members of the animal kingdom. Hayley works with a variety of mediums, including graphite pencils, acrylic paints and watercolours.

When not creating art, Hayley is an avid reader, a keen bushwalker and an enthusiastic gardener.

You can see more of Hayley's art or get in touch via her Instagram account at @hayleyclaireart.

Milton Keynes UK
Ingram Content Group UK Ltd.
UKHW010750180923
428890UK00004B/206